# TRAVELING WITH THE GHOSTS

# PRAISE FOR RADULESCU'S WORK

"In this poetry of passionate paradox, embodied thought becomes the solid clarity through which what we can't see is glimpsed."

–**Eleanor Wilner**

"Radulescu's poetry is an alchemy, a magic of restraint and exposure, revealing the machinations of our invisible feelings, motives, appetites, and fears."

–**Keith Flynn**

"Many native English speaking poets don't have such a supple and sensitive ear to the music of our language."

–**Annie Finch**

"Radulescu's poems are rich in connotations, metaphysically profound in some great unlocatable fashion. […] It's a dark poetry shining with the ecstasy of the imagination let loose, a triumph of being, a war against banality."

–**David Dodd Lee**

# TRAVELING WITH THE GHOSTS

STELLA VINITCHI RADULESCU

ISBN: 978-1-949039-25-2

Orison Books
PO Box 8385
Asheville, NC 28814
www.orisonbooks.com

Distributed to the trade by Itasca Books
1-800-901-3480 / orders@itascabooks.com

Cover art: "Woman Clothed in the Sun" (1985) by Faith
Wilding. Mixed media on paper, framed. 22 ¼ x 30
inches / 56.5 x 76.2 cm. Courtesy of the artist and Anat
Ebgi. Photo by Michael Underwood.

Manufactured in the U.S.A.

ORISON
BOOKS

# Contents

*And there was another noise, that of my life become the life of this garden as it rode the earth of deeps and wildernesses.*

**–Samuel Beckett,** *Molloy*

**first wave**     I take it

in my heart

nothing blue     not yet—

could you figure out the color

    of this hour

light hardens     your statue

rises in the air

put your cross away     once

      I walked from nowhere

to nowhere

    breathing was simple as

simple as death

**from neverness**     tomorrow

rises & like the river time runs

on my lips

hands grow & I teach silence

to children of dust to children

of wind


who came with apples & without—

you cannot see the void

with open eyes

the shark your friend tells you the truth


one life two lives the ocean rolls

in you—

you are redeemed  going away

& coming back

with the weather     : I hear your steps

along the shore     cast off a tear

it will rain

**drought**


the sun in the window

I read Šalamun    New York

is burning

it will    it did    you want

pistachios my little god

of everything

growing on Earth    it grew—

grew into drought or

something new

new & happy

like your face

when it's raining

**crossroad**

what do you mean by meaning

cric cric answers

the cricket

frogs are frozen     looking for a symbol

for god

I need a sentence to bring them

back to life

I don't have a pen     five fingers

that's it—

the only way to Paradise

is not to ask

**invocation**

those eyes you love

the violet eyes

of Spring     the girl

descending

the hill     or Spring

itself in violent

wind—

let me clean the air

with a vowel

or two     & start

the healing     can you be

more human

Death

as we are flying now on our

broken

      wings

**day one**

time to say yes

to your body the hour clicks

in your eyes

flakes    whispers    parts

of you    smell of spring    rushing

to an end    : one move

one dream

one disappearance


*


Adam the eagle & Eve the flying

redemption written in the air so sweet

the coming to a second

death

humans by name    little gods hidden

behind

the world wasn't here when

I was born     it came with me :

I am ahead

looking for a place to land


        *


we go in pairs like suns over the river

slowly melting into each other as night

consigns us to silence

and growing

inside ourselves     interior of a shell     the prayer

free of words the old cathedral sinks

in its own blood


        *


I peeled the truth     a corpse

inside

me in my own words

surfacing death dispersing air
follow the leaf

the view is nothing but the flight

between you & me

we've forgotten the day :

stay by your night stay by your

emptiness

it will call you     enable you to rise
fabulous speech near extinction—

this is how shadow by shadow

& void by void I put together

a new sentence

**a woman walks across the night**


she is coming from where the road ends

from where the wind stops

she in my flesh I open all doors

her carcass

beautiful bones left in the sun

a gift for my death oh, bonheur—


I am feeling the joy I go straight

into her eyes

to cut a piece of sky

*tear me up*     / that was her language

in my mouth /

I lacked words to bury her

in my yard


a woman walks across the night

on top

so bright

she carries the lamp brushes off

darkness

the image opens its eyes
Annunciation?

*a word from which you could have died*

**from your *book of hours***


is my body alive     or

half alive or     you see what you

want to see

a body alive or

imagine a figure from your *book of hours*

silent lips

not to disturb the coming

into being     I am craving

my flesh

the womb of the earth

giving birth

to the unknown child

**I hung my poem in a tree**

& bent my head under

the gloomy sky     a noise like

swarming dreams

a rush of bees—

bones are alive & loud who knows

the price of being &

the price of death     I don't have wings

but I can fly with all the leaves

the birds the clouds

I speak your language god

& you speak mine

stay tuned there is much more to say

come closer     eye

you river

of light

**first call**

call me alive among waves

of death

and breathless words moving

away


call me from where trees are spelling

my name     leaf by leaf

& sound by sound


a sign heraldic blows to life

the metaphor

survives

**in praise of spring**

there are small tender leaves

at the end of a branch

a luminous twig

eyes    piping hot in the grass

the snail looks happy—

it's Spring

a song cuts the silence

in two

there are dark-blue hills

in deep meditation    the burden

of a new joy—

the swan floats in the air

a template of an old

god

the poem ends    the heart

wakes up

to gather the crumbs

## with Rilke

on the
road
I see a
body
cut
in four
but
only
one
part
is moving
ahead
a cosmic
view
o,
angels—
and where
the prayer
goes—
you in
yourself
small as
a flake of
snow
huge as
the word
you say
it

**describe a rock** & feel

the lightness of the world

    one sound
two sounds

    butterflieswords—

    rivers are
  for cleaning the void

between your soul & your
      tongue

do not compare do not open
      the gate

    do not swallow your god

**history of something**


come secretly come in vain come
like a river a shadow

stepping hard
& flowing
over what should have been our

last day—
last & lasting forrever     I'll find you
a name

come to us from where we've
departed
so far away there is a shape

a human shape of two entangled
bodies come

from nowhere the ocean
the tide
come

near to separate us     a god inventing
his own
death

**ghost love**


coming from where we haven't

arrived     tears

freeze on the road


we've been brothers & sisters

lovers

squirrels & stars


the domain of living     things

to be & things to die:


the voice of the drowned man

surfaces us—

**only words**

so late

the coming to this : don't think

just talk

the rotten smell is brought by

quiet winds

on quiet pages :

let me move to the right & touch

your lips o, vastness

of one sound

*

you told me the story & I said

enough don't want to hear

the end     to pick up

dead stars

we were walking

the dangerous path

of our little lives only words

could carry so much

love

## remembrance

this is time     ravaging

hot inescapable clock

steaming the earth

the hour washed away by delicate

hands the foam

of our lives

blended

with your stillness

the blueness of the

world

hills darkening on your tongue

: silence is creeping up     a huge

empty mouth

I remember being    who knows—

I should dump you into this

nothingness

**through my hair the wind**

      speaks years     years

& months
            the ancient house

is coming to life

      not because I am here

or there     eternal or digging

my grave

      the meaning    slips

                   away
take me river

        to my first day

**remind me**

remind me black herald

that I am still on earth

naked like stones

washed

by the moon

your own image growing

in me

the wrong the white wing

I feel it now

fluttering in the wind

**traveling with the ghosts**


we are full of hope traveling

                  with our ghosts

suitcases & all

leaving home at night returning

with the sun


can't tell

if it happens to be

if the butterflies are back and

the lilac in blossom


I am warming up the place for

your beautiful death


*this is a love poem for you*

*who came at the window*

*winter heart*

*and a train of stars*

**breaking off the rhyme**

the show is on our love

back

years ago when it started—

a shrewd gnome

turned off the clock     *I have*

*to write it down*


yes or no     are these your steps

in the late September rain


a glitch in the count of days &

galaxies & souls

we were fastened tightened to a long sunny road

sheep like little gods

grazing at night


*roads are made to dreamily walk on*

*to end the story to break off*

*the rhyme*

**erotica**

what took so long to get
here

nine months nine centuries

of sweat & sweet

flowering     ghostly

stamens carried away by

the wind     : leaf

to leaf &

mouth to mouth     a hungry

moon steps in—

               stop the flow

we are as happy as our

words

I'll be you     remembrance

stigma     & you from

far away sowing

hours     scattering

loose

whatever remains

**spring rain**

I happen to be    to be there

in tiny places

tiny hidden places on earth

gathering pieces of sun

seconds & minutes

for the feast

of the year    : years left on empty

tables    —hunger &

innocence—

I was enormous at times pregnant

with the moon thirsty

for blood

a scream in my mouth that will

never end    —bones are

for holding the cross—o dear all of you,

do you smell fire in my flesh

I was fleshy I was bony falling &

climbing     : a butterfly a rat

and then

I took the shape of a cloud     rain
pouring from my chest

**second creation**

yes, the sculpture closed its eyes

a man a woman

who knows the gender of time


who molded us as such

ready to exchange

life for death


so far no answer     the trembling hand

planets & other species

roaming around—

soon

I'll find out


soon is now


*I was already there*

*in the space above     molding*

*the statue*

**evening blues**

the body rushes

to the river     lips

in the blue

light of one last

spring


birds

in the air

looking for a place

to nest—


flesh burns flesh     space

    burns space teaching us

    the fire:

    longing

for a rhyme?     what is the word

    for *love*?

## leaves birds grass

I, the one you love the only

one left aside from the storm

the big wave of light

how

I fit in your eyes

& you wanted me to open

my arms as dead as I was there is

no end

I conspired with the

stars     touch me touch

you

said with all the words growing

around leaves birds grass

## morphine

what else besides
what it is     Spring is falling

from the sky     we are hungry
     wounded blind     take
each word as it comes

I count my fingers miss
     my wings     no eyes

either for the swans     mother
says don't cry just don't     we were

chained to our lives inhaling
the rhyme     somebody plays
     the guitar—

God, I am so pleased with
my wounds

     blood on my tongue is
building the moon

**elegy**

the past is dying on the

future's tongue    : taste of fire

cities covered

in dust    colors

down to flat white—don't add


a rhyme    a cat a butterfly

the hour gets stuck

in the air

I want you dear mother to turn

me up-side down

**fragmentarium**


the bloody boots are boots for human feet
    to go ahead & to inspire peace up in the
        sky

and down under the tree stop stop saying
    this

your inspiration stinks your mind is
caught in heavy sounds
        bullets for the living

    there is an army in your room inhaling you
from top to top
        o, and this sentence

    it's snowing hard in town
nobody sleeps with snowy eyes let me tell you
        a story

with a cat going crazy for the rat
            cric cric the heart—
something stops & something goes on

    o god is it you who didn't come to heal
the wound
        or else . . .

**interval**

Picasso on the wall plays

with the sun

a woman smiles and waves

to me

: from the other side

what is invisible

speaks loud and stretches

beautiful wings

between time & time between

me & me bells

are tolling the splendor

of *I*

**death of a sonnet or how I gave birth to the sun**

### 1.

what's next     hard to say

even harder to write     a ball of fire

turned to ash

the page

the body flows down the creek

say something

make a wish on one thing     it will grow

& reach the sun     *some words are taking care*

*of our lives*

### 2.

forgetful time

the sea up to my throat     mother

knew the secret

and pushed me out of darkness     "aïe

paloma blanca"

a woman goes back to the shore

and swimming at night

keeps one word on her tongue

    : the last drop of light

**it was mid-winter or mid-fall**

we were captured as in a

spider web

words we never

said

& shining

dead


bring food & your hands

to set the table

in the air

so birds can start

the feast of

spring


mortality is all we need

**statuary**


the shape of my tongue

turns
     to the shape of a stone     winter white

& calm

days called nights     nobody

moves around with full legs

the landscape evolves     we talk

          loud & crisp

my styrofoam head hangs from silence—

the wasp caught
                    by its stinger

**a poem in the air**

the day before I was born

the park was empty—

a poem in the air     the swan

in full dailylight

four winds shifted the sun

squared off

the song

the coffin on the grass

**pagan prayer**

*How sad the flesh!*

–Stéphane Mallarmé

what is unspeakable comes

on foot

tramples down the grass

I feel like opening hundreds

of eyes and stepping

on my body

: inside

a scream    next door the light—

dead etymology and broken

sounds

the hand can't say *hand* the heart

can't spell its name

I worship the night & the hollow

face of the moon    O, God

open the route

cut a mouth in this desert

**given**

you can have these

words step on them

sleep on them take

them home let them

speak to you tell

stories paint you in

blue so hungry for

    your eyes to see them

    as such so hungry for

    your hands to touch

    them all    the way you

    touch a friendly

    corpse

**grace comes sometimes**

how dark the cloud    how low

the sky

he washed his hands down

by the creek

April fifteen    —the dog sleeps

his sleep—

he took a picture

& I smiled    grace comes

sometimes

wearing a yellow dress and

two big wings

I was supposed to fly

but I didn't

**and one last landscape**

pretend
   you
      are
         alive
           and up
              in full
                 sight
                  worms
              take
        a
     short
   break
  grass
will
   grow
      else-
        where

**still life with apples & a cup of tea**


I talk to you from my bed hanging
from the ceiling hanging
from a dream

my grandmother smiles from
her framed picture
next to the book open at page twenty-five

where somebody wrote a poem

*still life with apples . . .*

or maybe he didn't even write it
& ate the apples & drank
the tea

the yellow cup & the knife in the kitchen
pierce the eye—

in front of me    infinity    a thought
looking for a place to settle down .

today is gone & yesterday again

I am thirsty I am sad    the day lingers
on the couch
the hallway then    ends in the garden

I hear a step    a noise    & I think of you
living with the stars

**a solitary thought**


a solitary thought erupts into

the dusty town     o, be a butterfly—said

the child with one big eye

any many days to count—

the picture of the sky

ephemeral

like time


a single history or many more

the fluctuations

of light     o, be the ocean steaming

cleaning up the dust

like hope

that bubble ready to explode

**how I dream (1)**


the poem stands in front

of me     : a mountain

                dispersing
   the fog

we don't sleep like animals

   in total
                darkness—
what to expect

        a flower
a delicate
        hand     an empty

page     longing     for words

while words like birds

       in autumn wind

are leaving

**how I dream (2)**


more questions

swirling on the wall     how

could I be so full

of me

and empty

all the way     as angels

frighten me with snow

& lightness—

                    I wake up
heavy

the heaviness of words

**disappearance**     traveling

east

one foot behind the time

    o rivers

o creeks with the smell

of departing

I hear steps in the garden

    who is there

looking for me
        —you    hour

I can't follow you

        in your flight

hide me    hide me

    on your tongue    a word

to be said    a word    to be

loved

**what is light**

in a dream I was

taken to a sinful

place

don't look back said

the Master but

I did &

grew as a plant

touching

the ceiling to escape

darkness     what is

light if not

one more word for

resurrection

**am I from here**     —a sudden

chime—

terminal season in eyes all eyes

blinking together—

    togetherness like

a conspiracy
                  a crime

    I wake up early and asking

questions     whose turn

whose name     there are faces

    around &

shadows in the air     I shake yours

    with both hands

**in sweat & fear** the body

flies     would be an angel

would be a snake


come closer     you from

the region of life

   what

could I say to you

                no words

allowed beyond the fence—


two worlds

are fighting winding

down     set up the weather

whisper my name


we'll meet one day halfway

to death

**I dream in you** and start

to build small worlds

around     a shoal of fish

a nesting bird     tulips

in yellow light

            slow clouds

on the move like slow

moving

elephants     a house     a pond

in which I sink

: a tear     too shy or

too heavy

you took it back into your

eye

**that wounded hour**

    of the Earth circling

a body    hawk style &

    calmly descending on us


the dead army seen from

    afar    like a white field—

inflorescence—    we breathe

    we breathe

stepping on our long dead

    dreams

**ecstasy on the road to hell**


is it the song the true one & fog spreading

over the land

with a taste of happiness


I am nothing but a dream clean & caged

many others bleed in me—


going nowhere like a flying soul

I haven't arrived

before dawn

to break off the rule of Ascension

**adoration of the magi**

objects have a soul

you think they don't & trample them

down & give them names

when names get lost in time—

look up

the scene    the painting    the world

in adoration

I moved the sign from white to black

and I don't know—

ask me why

just ask

the Magi kneeling at the door

with gifts of life & hope    how real

the feeling on the crumpled

page    —the joy

is coming    the mind

makes monsters     monsters

of love

**the prophet of the war the snake**

the prophet of the war

the snake

wakes up & crawling on my neck

& carving planets & stones

makes everything

square


there are children on the street

and squirrels in trees

parts & bones

underground and some hope for

another round:


said the mouth loud & clear

like an open

tomb

**driving north**

here are some thoughts I am trying
to spell out

just in case

light keeps changing direction
milk keeps pouring for the unborn child

I am looking for facts

real facts big names     a supernova a storm

vintage love

a man with a pink tie     : make it black
said the mortician

on our way to heaven

**sanctuary**

*He* didn't allow me to be

the root

& the flower

choose one     when

where

& who makes rules to break

in pieces

my body

I came from far away to build

a sky a sea

& many waves & doors

to keep us far

from being whatever

we are

: I am

I was :

and my eyes cling to this night

**texts & paratexts**

*How can one write nothing?*

–Jacques Derrida


it's terrifying      truth

the rapture

here      the burning house

seconds & minutes

they whisper        still alive & clean

& rushing

on the page

: the funeral

the daring mind


*

and so we go ahead and write

what hands can do

what brain can brew

the comma separates two worlds

not far or close not right or wrong:

correct the manuscript     the setting

on the page

the phonetics of wind:

a line too long     a life

too short

*oh, you*

*the perfect Word—*


\*


in rhymes the night

sets up

a sky

and dreams as metaphors

of life

are breaking off

the lines

*

should god talk loud

or soft to tame

such times—

lower the sky deepen

the pond

jump into your death &

come to me

alive

**dusk dusk**

find

a rhyme ask

our gods to light

a candle

the page lies

blank

too far the stars

too deep the grave

speak     your

life

a word can burn

forever

**and who is He**

     and where to look to find

no answer

     but the question—

he slept his life & then awake

       knelt in my heart as

kneeling will have dug

           a grave—

     some people still are calling

  me    dividing parts

    & sounds

—what do I love & what belongs

to me—    my fingers touch

    & touch your face

and touching

      is one answer

## God's hunger

she keeps falling and is midnight

the station in the blue light

of the blue snow

—which train—

she keeps going down slowly

tightening her hair with a ribbon

of blood

calling me

my phone is dead a century ends

with a lost number

falling & asking the final

question

should I go on should I feed

more lives from the past

: God's hunger

not mine

**apocalyptic**

writing about something or

just writing—pretending beauty

while beauty soars

to stars—

a swallow flies in my chest

then makes a turn

leaves me here

alone

new & untouched     nothing

to be said twice

I open the gate & cry out

my name

**testament**

to forget or

to keep alive the world in its

    hinges    door

open door closed

            the tremolo

    between you

& me        the rope

& who is there on top

        the meaning
slips

away    or    living had

become
        a yesterday

the subject was erased

the breathing

        pinned to the wall

do you want to praise

the name
of the rose or

the rose itself     the blood

the blooming

**from clay to stars**


the distance grows by days

by nights      : who didn't

come—

      nobody

are we still waiting      let's sit

on the grass & mold

our love


a leg      an eye      a flower

      rouge—

who didn't sing—the *other*

voice

you took the shovel—

nobody

underground

we all are here      in full

sight      bodies

growing dusty to a luminous end

**the day I left**


the army of the dead watches us as we eat

breakfast and talk—

a cross rises to a sky of doubtful

forgiveness—


they have dew on their lips the sweat

of the grass

and soft eyes blinking at night


they are hiding their faces

their shining wounds     hands moving

the winds

across the sea—


sounds of war in the air I am not

the black angel

with his noisy sword nor the flower

with purple teeth

the woman you'd have loved

in times of peace—

the day I left was already a night

the stars were moving

backwards     our water our bread

were told

in no terrestrial voice

an insomniac god

was cleaning the place—

the sheep still grazing

in the yard

and songs like bees were passing

in large swarms

**like history a poem**

*I, too, sing America.*

*I am the darker brother.*

–Langston Hughes


cats sleep
close the door to the attic

the noise comes from my mouth
straight talk & sounds

of rage

humans drinking human
blood

& monsters wear the crown
*In God We Trust*

I am caged in words
like history:

voices     you     don't shiver
bury the corpses

the Evil     my yellow shoes—
yellow for the eternal

walk:     the TV zoom zoom

barbarians on the road

my neighbors hanging their clothes

the sun &
the clothesline    lines

lines—
disruption in time don't blink
stay tuned
keep thinking    fill up the void
a syllable is worth a life

& drink their milk babies are coming
babies like funeral stones    hey, joy

you've lost your *y*

a strike in Heaven    Dante
says is divine

**o night divine**

to catch the train & go

to my lost land

tigers in cages are praying for me


how I praise the occasion

to wear a crown—the understanding


the word *night* is my friend

    o night divine

came close & closer chasing

the day


mouth to mouth & verb to verb

I want to go crisp    icy-white

into forgetting

**ghost moon in my window**

travels the room

sits on my pillow

I inhale the dust the clumsiness

of its light

something is going on with

no future with

no past

who has blue eyes

teeth like candles I lit one

by one—

ahead of me my grave

is floating

in time

**under the shroud**


one more picture

    under the shroud

        the ghostly sky

            the nowhere clouds

the sun becoming stellar—

thinner the road    wooden

the heart

: it shelters us

           like in a mirror

we are & we are not

**blues (1)**

an angel lost his wings

by telling the truth

female or male

couldn't fly

or walk

on layers of light

which wasn't

light

nor darkness     soul

after soul

begging to let them in—

I am walking on snow as if

on lost dreams

**blues (2)**

music from the bones    : sleep

my heart     dream

as if already dead you're looking

for seasons looking

for spring

water dripping from closed

eyes

hands shivering the branches

the tree

a solitary thought pushes

the sky beyond

the words     here

& there

music from the bones

**diary page one**

evening in town

scary blue

my heart catches the last

drop of sun

what you don't see

the crumbling

the agony in clouds

what you don't hear

the marching

on the street


all the black angels

**diary page two**


going to page two I ate

an apple

I touched a star

a century collapsed


close one eye     the other

will blossom with

light

**nightly talk**

   deathless soul dying in me     innumerable

falling stars

which language do I speak bypassing

Ascension

touching the earth is all the rain needs

and love returns to its pit     gently

come to me fruit & flower

in one

**counting the falling stars**

there is a story with no end

& tiny lives ahead     you & me

& us the flow so dense

defaces

time

my duty is to wake at night

& count the falling stars cold meals

on the table

and no

we are not here yet     still digging

what

should have been said

a color blue

a sky around

& eyes like moons in freezing nights

**days & beyond**

the rapist is Time

crouched under my bed

of flowers
                    days

and beyond     they strike

at night melting my teeth

into vicious

sounds


: words chasing words

how quick my hand

is turning into a happy

branch

the logic of the flesh against

eternal night—

**before stillness**

before stillness before a flake

of snow before

the quiet drum

of evening

whose life exploded in the

field & made us

wonder

pray & tell to our children

stories of war

and freshly buried

bodies—

silence is leaking & we can hear

the stars

dropping dead in our

yard

**untitled**

a man    a life    a suicide

the sun is up

the language down

somebody came somebody leaves in a bag

*want to repeat that?*

: birds in long flocks

deserting

the sky

**you you the absolute fou**

I am dying in you     nothing

belongs to me

last move on an empty

stage:

blame me for all

I am

for all I am not

I wake up at night

& the day sits at the window

bird of prey:

don't harm my children

don't harm

my dreams

we were in brackets we were

in rhymes

linked by many dots

orphans

loosing each minute

a father or two

but who who      who are you mister
mister

the absolute fou

nailed on the wall

tick tick      and the white whale

swallows up      page after

page after

page

**flying east with the birds**

*Fly, bird, fly away; teach me to disappear!*

–Fernando Pessoa


we are flying east with the birds

the swallows the geese the hummingbirds

blessed by darkness

bones softened

by joy


soul to soul tighten in the air death

keeps us afloat     as we sleep

& don't sleep and speak

our secret language


we are flying East with the birds

the swallows the geese the hummingbirds

the moon is up     the page

slides down

no winds no waves could ever take us

to the end

**how to say yes** & open

the gate &

let the sun enter the body

& let the light

paint me in blue     I am

your sky & you are

mine

there is a reason for being

alive     I speak to you

in many languages &

still can't find

the final word to stop the

flow recurring—

can't spell it

out loud

**last judgment**

what it takes to die

    a life of course

time rushed    a horse

    a pint of blood

some had the chance to be

in front

calm down my soul

    the counting starts

backwards

**imprint**

my words devour me piece

by piece

  you child

don't come

in such voracious time—

they want me pure

naked whole

a carcass left right here

in the sun

I am considering the price—

a single page in black

& white

**epiphany**

behind my eyes a cloud opens

the gate

a child goes to the river

the hummingbird prays loud

to the unseen

god

some understanding comes from

a star

rowing the silence

we wrap our bones in plastic bags

sprinkle them with holy oil—

take for example

the spine

: the horizon

bent all the way down

**minus infinity**

it's a bird jumping

      to the sky:

let me be the eye & the sound


  : or the sun

taste of the apple roundness melting

     in my mouth

there is nothing else

to say

     the explosion is over

          *ineffable like death I am rising*

# Acknowledgments

*2River Review*: "blues (1)," "blues (2)"

*Asheville Poetry Review*: "remembrance," "ghost love"

*Balloons Literary Journal*: "I hung my poem in a tree"

*Cecile's Writers Magazine* (Netherlands): "counting the falling stars," "imprint"

*The Chattahoochee Review*: "breaking off the rhyme"

*Contemporary Poetry* (Vol. 2, 2015), ed. Deepak Chaswal & Pradeep Chaswal: "adoration of the magi"

*Every Writer*: "a solitary thought"

*Fiolet & Wing: An Anthology of Domestic Fabulism*: "still life with apples & a cup of tea"

*Five 2 One Magazine*: "a woman walks across the night," "untitled" (as "title down"), "stranger . . ."

*The Freeman*: "second creation"

*Gris-Gris Poetry Review*: "spring rain"

*The Inflectionist Review*: "minus infinity"

*JMWW*: "morphine"

*Literature Today*: "flying east with the birds"

*Midway Journal*: "pagan prayer"

*Misrepresented People: Poetic Responses to Trump's America*, ed. María Isabel Álvarez & Dante Di Stefano (NYQ Books, 2018): "like history a poem"

*The Muse*: "only words"

*The Orison Anthology* (Vol. 1, 2016): "the prophet of the war the snake," "traveling with the ghosts" (reprints)

*Otis Nebula*: "history of something"

*Scapegoat Review*: "evening blue," "traveling with the ghosts," "the prophet of the war the snake"

*Twyckenham Notes*: "nightly talk," "under the shroud"

*Visions International*: "driving north"

*Voice of Eve*: "fragmentarium," "erotica," "leaves birds grass"

*The Voices Project*: "from neverness"


The poems "remind me" and "apocalyptic" were translated into Serbian by Danijela Trajković and published in the following volumes: *22 вагона* [*22 Wagons*] (Istok Academia, Knjazevac, Serbia, 2018) and *TRAG* anthology, Narodna biblioteka "Danilo Kis."

# About the Author

Stella Vinitchi Radulescu was born in Romania. She left the country in 1983, at the height of the communist regime. She holds a PhD in French Language & Literature, and she was a professor of French at Loyola University and Northwestern University for many years. The author of numerous poetry collections published in the United States, France, Belgium, and Romania, Radulescu writes in three languages, though she does not translate any of her work between languages. In 2019, a volume of Luke Hankins's English-language translations of her French poetry, *A Cry in the Snow & Other Poems*, was published by Seagull Books. Orison Books released a collection of Radulescu's English-language work, *I Scrape the Window of Nothingness: New & Selected Poems*, in 2015.

# About Orison Books

Orison Books is a 501(c)3 non-profit literary press focused on the life of the spirit from a broad and inclusive range of perspectives. We seek to publish books of exceptional poetry, fiction, and non-fiction from perspectives spanning the spectrum of spiritual and religious thought, ethnicity, gender identity, and sexual orientation.

As a non-profit literary press, Orison Books depends on the support of donors. To find out more about our mission and our books, or to make a donation, please visit www.orisonbooks.com.

For information about supporting upcoming Orison Books titles, please visit www.orisonbooks.com/donate, or write to Luke Hankins at editor@orisonbooks.com.